OPTIONS TRADING CRASH COURSE

The Complete Crash Course Guide To Become A Top Trader. Easy Strategies And Investing Techniques To Make Money And Achieve Financial Freedom

Author:
AMERICA'S TRADING

Table of Contents

INTRODUCTION..**8**

SIGNS OF FINANCIAL SLAVERY 8

FINANCIAL FREEDOM 11

TRADING OPTIONS TO GAIN FINANCIAL FREEDOM....................... 14

WHAT YOU WILL LEARN IN THIS BOOK................................. 15

CHAPTER 1: HABITS, MINDSET, AND FOCUS...................18**

THE MINDSET IN OPTION TRADING 19

DECISION MAKING 20

RISK-TAKING 21

FLEXIBILITY 21

DOES MINDSET MATTER IN OPTIONS TRADING?......................... 22

TRAITS OF AN INDIVIDUAL WITH THE RIGHT MINDSET IN OPTIONS TRADING. 24

PATIENCE.. 24

DISCIPLINE.. 25

ABILITY TO MANAGE RISKS... 25

CHAPTER 2: WHY START OPTIONS TRADING 28**

OPTIONS PROVIDE LEVERAGE 28

OPTIONS ARE INEXPENSIVE.. 29

OPTIONS PRICES CHANGE IN BIG WAYS.................................. 29

OPTIONS HAVE A HIGHER ROI... 30

OPTIONS ARE FLEXIBLE... 31

OPTIONS ARE FAST 32

CHAPTER 3: THE BASICS OF OPTIONS TRADING AND WHAT IT IS

....**34**

WHAT IS OPTIONS TRADING?.. 34

CALL AND PUT 35

PRACTICAL EXAMPLE 36

HOW THE OPTIONS WORK 40

CHAPTER 4: HOW TO START WITH OPTIONS TRADING 44**

CHAPTER 5: THE MOST IMPORTANT TYPES OF OPTIONS TRADING 50

UNDERLYING ASSET 50

DIFFERENT TYPES OF OPTIONS 51

CREATED ON THURSDAYS...53

MINI OPTIONS 54

INDEX OPTIONS 54

BINARY OPTIONS...55

CHAPTER 6: STRATEGIES AND TIPS FOR OPTIONS TRADING........60

TIPS FOR OPTION TRADING 60

TRADING STRATEGIES 63

RESEARCH..66

HAVE A PLAN 67

CHAPTER 7: LINGO LEARNING 68

ASK..68

ASSIGNMENT 69

AT THE MONEY 69

BID PRICE 69

BREAK-EVEN POINT...69

CALL 69

COMMISSION..70

DELTA 70

EARLY EXERCISE 70

EXERCISE...70

EXPIRATION DATE 70

IN THE MONEY (CALL)...71

IN THE MONEY (PUT) 71

INDEX OPTIONS 71

INTRINSIC VALUE 71

LEAP 71

LEGS 72

LONG...72

MARGIN REQUIREMENT 72

OPTION CHAIN 72

OUT-OF-THE-MONEY 72

PREMIUM 73

PUT 73

ROLL A LONG POSITION.. 73

ROLL A SHORT POSITION... 73

SERIES 74

SHORT 74

STRIKE PRICE 74

TIME VALUE 75

TIME DECAY 75

UNDERLYING 75

WEEKLY 75

CHAPTER 8: COVERED CALL STRATEGIES, EXAMPLES 78

COVERED CALLS 79

EXAMPLES 80

SELLING OPTIONS STRATEGY: BUY IT BACK 82

OPTIONS THAT EXPIRE IN THE MONEY WILL BE EXERCISED 84

STRATEGY: PROTECTED PUTS.. 84

DIVIDEND WARNING 85

CHAPTER 9: VOLATILITY..86

WHAT IS VOLATILITY?.. 86

STRATEGIES FOR A VOLATILE MARKET 89

CHAPTER 10: STRANGLES AND STRADDLES 94

CHAPTER 11: CREDIT SPREADS AND DEBIT SPREADS EXPLAINED
..100

CREDIT SPREADS.. 101

TYPES OF CREDIT SPREADS 102

PROS AND CONS OF CREDITS SPREADS... 105

DEBIT SPREADS.. 105

TYPES OF DEBIT SPREADS 107

PROS AND CONS OF DEBIT SPREADS 111

CHAPTER 12: IRON CONDOR EXPLAINED AND EXAMPLES 112

BENEFITS OF THE IRON CONDOR SPREAD.. 114

RISKS OF THE IRON CONDOR SPREAD 114

CHAPTER 13: COMMON MISTAKES NOT TO DO IN OPTIONS TRADING **116**

FAILURE TO UNDERSTAND THE TRADE 117

IMPATIENCE..118

FAILURE TO DIVERSIFY...118

GETTING TOO CONNECTED WITH A CERTAIN COMPANY...............119

INVESTMENT TURNOVER 119

TIMING THE MARKET 119

TRADING WITH EMOTIONS 120

SETTING UNREALISTIC EXPECTATIONS 120

USING BORROWED MONEY 121

CONCLUSION **122**

Introduction

Financial freedom. Many seek it but few have it. That is because the secrets behind obtaining it are closely guarded by those who have it. This book is about exposing one true and reliable way that you can earn the financial security and independence you need to take control of the way you live your daily life.

Signs of Financial Slavery

The first active step needed to get started on a journey to financial freedom is acknowledging that you are not financially stable or free. This is a hard pill for some people to swallow and so they avoid acknowledging it even with the overwhelming evidence to support the state. Facing this fact is not about demeaning your integrity or bring you down. It is about giving you a foundation to start with so that you can build the financial security you need. This knowledge is needed to show you where you currently stand financially and what your resources are so that you can develop a plan to get where you need and want to be.

The following conditions are those that chain many people to financial slavery:

- Living paycheck to paycheck. People who live this way do not have an emergency fund and typically have accompanying credit card debt because they need to subsidize their expenses, which are higher than their income. Many people live this way. In fact, more than 40% of American households could not cover a $400 expense such as medical bills or car repairs if it came up unexpectedly in 2017.

- Not having enough saved up to sustain their lifestyle if they were to lose their job. People such as these do not have enough money accumulated to take time away from working on a daily basis. This is the reason why most people are in careers and jobs that bring them no joy. They need the salary to keep a roof over their heads and food in their belly and so, they deal with the circumstances that make them unhappy.

- Not being able to pursue the activities and adventures that bring happiness while still saving and accumulating wealth. These types of people are stuck in a cycle of trading their daily hours for money while still being unable to enjoy the money that they earn because it is not enough to allow them this enjoyment and still pay the bills.

- Having inflexible schedules. Most people are stuck in a cycle of working every day and going home to come back to work the next day. They have to give this time to earn an income and therefore, become chained to their jobs.

- Not being able to retire comfortably at the desired age. The world over, the average age for retirement is 65 years old. However, many people are not expected to live even 20 years past that age. That does not live much time to enjoy a life free of accumulating wealth. The sadder fact is that most people do not retire with enough money saved up to enjoy the things that they want after retirement. Some others still have to work a job even after this age to sustain themselves. People who are financially free are able to retire at the age that they want rather than one that is dictated by someone else. They also have the capital available to do the things they want to do and still have income coming to them on a more passive basis.

- Spending more money than earned. This results because people want to live the lifestyle that they want but cannot afford or people needing to subsidize their income to cater to their needs. To build wealth, you cannot have more money going out than coming in. Signs that your spending exceeds your income include having a budget based on your salary, having an expense list that exceeds your net income, carrying a balance on your credit card, having rent or mortgage that is more than 30% of your net income and buying things to impress or keep up with other people.

Are you slave to your finances? Would you like to use your time in other ways while still earning a steady and growing income? Can you use the extra income to develop the lifestyle you want?

Answering yes to any of these income questions or relating to even just one of the conditions stated above means you can use the advice and strategies outlined in this book.

Financial Freedom

Having financial freedom is more than just having a 6-month emergency fund saved up and your debt cleared. Financial freedom means taking control of your time and finances so that you can do the things that you want to do rather than what your bank account figure dictates. Being financially free means you do not need to trade your time for money.

To be able to gain this financial freedom, you need to have financial security. Financial security is the condition whereby you support the standard of living you want now and in the future by having stable sources of income and other resources available to you. That means not living paycheck to paycheck. It means not having to worry about where your next dollar will come from. It means having a huge weight lifted off your shoulders because you know there are resources that you can leverage to get the things that you want and need.

People who have financial freedom are also financially independent. Financial independence is the state of having personal wealth to maintain the lifestyle and the standard of living you want without actually having to trade your daily hours for money. The assets and resources that you have generated will gain that income for you so that your income remains far greater than your expenses. In essence, being financially independent means that you can go for a prolonged period of time without trading time for money and still have the standard of living that you want. That you can go on a year-long vacation and still be secure in the knowledge that your wealth is still growing.

To be financially independent, you have to have:

- An emergency fund that can sustain your lifestyle for an extended period of time (years).
- Assets that produce income for you on a daily, weekly, monthly, and yearly basis.
- Very little or zero debt.

Very few people on the planet are financially secure and independent. In fact, more than 1 billion people live in extreme poverty. In 2015, it was estimated that more than 10% of the global population lived on less than US$1.90 per day.

Despite these statistics, there is hope. This hope comes from the fact that this statistic goes down every year. In fact, in 2019 less than 8% of the global population lived in extreme poverty. This is largely attributed to the fact that people being more educated about their options and are not just accepting of these poor circumstances.

Despite this improvement, most of the global population still trades their time for an hourly wage. The income earned from this is not sustainable nor will it allow them to live the standard of life that they would like. They will not be able to retire comfortably. There is no power or security in living this way. People who are financially free have learned and harnessed the power of passive income. Passive income is wealth that is generated from little to no effort or earned in the way of exchanging time for money over the long term. While it might take a massive amount of time and effort to establish in the beginning, passive income allows you to earn money even while you sleep with little to no daily effort required for its maintenance.

The beauty of passive income is that it is not only limited to one income bracket or portion of the population. Anyone can develop passive income as long as they develop the right mindset and is willing to put in the time and effort to learn and be consistent in pursuing this standard of living.

Trading Options to Gain Financial Freedom

Trading options has the great potential to be a form of passive income. This is the complete opposite of active income, which is what most people engage in. Active income is one where a person invests time in exchange for money. Passive income allows you to still enjoy your time as you dictate while earning money. It comes to you on automatic even while you sleep. While it usually takes time, effort, and maybe monetary input at the beginning, over the long-term, if done right, you can sustain the lifestyle you want if you put forth that investment now.

Passive income:

- Gives you the platform to gain financial stability, security, and independence.
- Gives you the freedom to do whatever you wish with your time without the worry of sustaining your financial life.
- Gives you the freedom to pursue the career, hobbies, and other activities you love and enjoy rather than having to trade your time for money.
- Allows you to secure your financial future, thus getting rid of your worry, stress, and anxiety in that department.
- Gives you the flexibility to live and work from anywhere in the world, typically. The bonus of this means you get to travel if that is a pursuit you would like to take on while still earning.

Trading options can give you the benefits listed above and thus, light the way to your financial freedom.

What You Will Learn in This Book

My goal when writing this book was to show you how you can take control of your finances, pay off your debt and live life on your own terms using one powerful strategy.

As I mentioned above, having a growth mindset means that you openly receive information from other people to better yourself and your financial life. I am sharing my knowledge with you in this insightful guide because I have implemented these same strategies with tremendous success. It is not a perfect system, but it is one that works well if done right and consistently.

Before I invite you to delve in, let me say this… To gain the most benefit from reading the information to come, you need to cultivate the growth mindset mentioned above. You have to also treat this like a business, not a side gig. This is not a hobby nor something that you are just dabbling in. Make the effort and time you invest count. Make it consistent and be persistent. Set a schedule and work on this every day. Make goals for yourself and give yourself a timeline for your accomplishments. Stay focused and committed.

The world's wealth is majorly divided into a small part of the population. Only that small percentage has financial freedom. You can put yourself and your family in that small percentile using this method for passive income. I have faith that you can do it as long as you put in that initial effort. The question is – do you believe that you can do too? Can you envision yourself as the person who has attained financial freedom in the future and is living the life you want?

Answer *YES* to both these questions and believe in that answer, I implore you!

Now, without further ado, let's jump into this invaluable guide so that you can start the future you desire today.

CHAPTER 1:

Habits, Mindset, and Focus

In this topic, we will focus on mindset and how it impacts option trading both in positive and negative ways. To start with, it is very important to understand what mindset is and the types in case of any. Mindset is, therefore, refers to the assumptions, notions, and beliefs that a person has or the manner in which they view incidents and interpret them.

Mindsets exist in two different forms, that is, a growth mindset and a fixed mindset. A fixed mindset is where a person will always have certain thoughts and views towards something, and in case of problems, they believe they can find a solution to them. A growth mindset is that one will view life or any situation from different angles and points of view. To them, they would always find solutions to problems by all means. Those people with a growth mindset usually act excited and always ready to learn or develop new skills that will help them come up with solutions. Those with fixed mindsets usually do not grow mentally and in other spheres as they fix themselves to certain positions in life without any intent to change.

The Mindset in Option Trading

Before venturing into options trading, the kind of mindset that you have towards it is very vital. This is because the sale and purchase of securities need to be thought about carefully least one makes losses rather than profits. Apart from that, options trading for a long time has become a hard nut to crack too many as they believe that it is a very hard investment. With this kind of mindset, it would be hard for someone to overcome the various hurdles that are associated with this investment. When faced with problems, one can even quit if they have a fixed mindset or make poor decisions that will sire consecutive losses in the long run.

This, therefore, means that there is a strong relationship between one's mindset and trading options. This is because the mindset is the one that can either determine losses or profits. The following are some instances where the mindset is related to options trading:

Decision Making

Like any other kind of investment, options trading also has a series of situations that require one to make vital decisions that will decide the future of the investment. When buying or selling options (securities), the price is usually determined for a certain period of time. When buying options, one always has to make a decision that will allow them to make a profit when they decide to sell in the future. On the first go, one might unexpectedly go on a loss if the decision made was not so good. This makes many lose hope and have the mindset that options trading is a complicated investment, which is not the case.

A person who has a fixed mindset will always view options trading to be complicated and very hard to venture into. With this mindset, it would be very hard for them to make a sane decision at any given point. This may cost them by making the run into consecutive losses to the point of quitting options trading.

On the other hand, a person who has a growth mindset will try to look for solutions for the problem and the way in which they can go about it to make profits once again.

This is a person who will learn from the first poor decision and focus on making a better decision the next time they trade. This person, with time, will have learned all the required skills to trade and make profits. This, therefore, proves to us that mindset has got a very strong link to options trading.

Risk-Taking

Every investment is characterized by various risks that are associated with it. Options trading is not an exception, as it also has many risks that are capable of negatively impacting the investment. One of the major risks is making losses and getting major disappointments. Another risk is being bankrupt, which is a result of the chain of losses. Despite all these risks that endanger the sustenance of your investment, the mindset you have will always determine whether it will succeed or fall.

A person with a fixed mindset in this kind of situation might easily give up. This is because the individual will view options trading as a losing investment that does them no good at all. It would be even more dangerous if one continues trading with this kind of mindset. This is because they would never expect anything less than losses. On the other hand, a person with a growth mindset will take the loss as a steppingstone. They would then use these instances to come up with new approaches and skills that will help them overcome this risk. In the end, this person will definitely make profits and enjoy the investment as he will be well equipped with the necessary skills for risk management.

Flexibility

In options trading, one is supposed to always be flexible, just like any other kind of investment out there. Options trading has got different terms and conditions that possibly change over time. Before making a sale or purchase of options, one should be well conversant and equipped with the knowledge of the trade. Failure to abide by these conditions might find your trade to be obsolete and might lead you to losses. Some of these terms and conditions are usually harsh and very hard to abide by them, thus might even require you to change the trading approach you use in order to remain valid. Having the right mindset is also very vital in strictly ensuring that your trade is in line with the set conditions.

If you have negative reasoning and a fixed mindset towards the set conditions and terms, then you might not be able to succeed in the trade. You will tend to focus on the negatives that they are doing to the trade rather than how it would impact it positively. This will, therefore, make you drift focus from making profits through options sales and purchases to change in the conditions. This will thus guarantee you a series of losses in the investment. On the other hand, for a person who has a positive and growth mindset, the change of the terms and conditions will be a non-issue to them. This is because they will easily devise new trading approaches that will fit the conditions and continue making profits. This thus depicts a great relation between the mindset of a person and options trading.

Does Mindset Matter in Options Trading?

In life, if not investments such as options trading, there are various challenges that we face as we carry out our activities. These challenges face everyone, and some will comfortably overcome them while some will just whine and cry over them without looking for any possible solutions. This all depends on the person's mindset, either a growth mindset or a fixed mindset. A person with a fixed mindset will just give up on life and make no step in trying to count these problems. On the other hand, an individual with a growth mindset will think over the problem and come up with a solution using their skills to overcome this problem.

In terms of investments and options trading, in particular, nothing is different, as the same also applies. Having a fixed mindset makes you only cry over problems you face in the trade rather than come up with solutions. It is, therefore, clear that someone who has a growth mindset will definitely do better in trading as compared to the one with a fixed mindset. Individuals with fixed mindsets are always said to seem to seek approval. They will even engage in trying to prove themselves in the trading and fail to look for more information as they might be wrong. In any situation, there is always the call for confirming their intelligence, character, or personality. They also evaluate situations that they are in to determine if they will succeed or not.

Having a growth mindset usually leads to the quest for more knowledge and the desire to make new discoveries and work hard. Apart from that and most importantly, having a growth mindset will make one be able to tackle challenges, thus grow in all spheres of life comfortably. Individuals with a growth mindset will take failure when they try as a learning experience, which will eventually lead them to change, growth, and success. When it comes to option trading, they will not see losses they make as disappointments or losing it in life generally. They will instead see it as a challenge and opportunity to grow and put in place strategies that will help solve the issue. With this spirit, it would be very easy to conduct options trading and make very big profits. From this, we can, therefore, come up with a conclusion that mindset is very critical in options trading. It may determine whether you are going to make a profit from your trade or losses. It also depicts the resilience level you have that will enable you to keep up the options trading despite any problems that might come your way. Apart from that, mindset matters because it will depict the future of your options trade. It will determine if it will grow and be better or worst. This, therefore, calls for every individual who does options trading to have the right mindset, and they will be able to do well in it.

Traits of an Individual with the right Mindset in Options Trading

Having the right mindset in options trading is something that one expresses in the way they do their trading activities. In the current financial markets, options are very versatile and vital instruments. For an individual to trade in these options, they should have the right mindset that will make them succeed in the long last. This, therefore, means that they should possess certain personality traits. These traits include:

Patience

Patience is one of the qualities that are possessed by options traders. Investors that are patient will always be willing and ready to wait until the market provides the right chances and opportunities. This is opposed to always trying to reap big profits from every movement in the market. Traders will, therefore, always be seen to be idling while busy keeping an eye on the market as they wait for a perfect moment to either exit or enter a trade. Other traders who might be armatures or generally not serious with the trade would quickly do trades, and due to their impatience, they will easily exit or enter trades. An individual with the right mindset in options trading should also be patient.

Discipline

In order to be a successful options trader, one should be much disciplined. Many activities in options trading, such as looking for opportunities, forming strategies and adhering to them, and even venturing into the right trade, require much discipline. A common example of indiscipline that happens too many is doing as others do. An opinion given by someone else is never trustworthy since they might have done research from a different point of view compared to yours. This might lead to losses that you cannot blame them for it. Discipline will, therefore, entail you devising your own independent trading strategies that will work with you, and thus you will be a successful options trader.

Ability to Manage Risks

Options trading is characterized by an array of risks. Therefore, it is very important to be able to recognize and identify the number of risks that you have at a given time. It is thus very vital for options traders to put in place appropriate measures that will help in controlling the risks. For example, a short-term trader would make frequent losses in their trades;

thus, they need certain risk management approaches to count this. With these tactics, you will be able to count the risks and be a successful options trader.

CHAPTER 2:

Why Start Options Trading

I t's useful to know why we are trading options in the first place. The fact that they are cheap, is only one factor to consider. We are going to look at some of the specific benefits that come with trading options. Knowing what they are is going to help you make the right investment decisions.

Options Provide Leverage

When you buy an options contract, you control 100 shares of stock for the lifetime of that option. An option is a tool that allows you to control those shares of stock without paying the full price for them. For example, Apple may be trading at $200 a share. An options contract on Apple might cost $125 for a particular strike price. Had I actually purchased the shares; the cost would be $200/share x 100 shares = $20,000. So, for 0.625% of the price of the shares, I can control the shares for the time until the options contract either expires or I sell it.

Options Are Inexpensive

OK, this is kind of a restatement of the point above, but to buy shares you need a lot of money. Yes, you could buy one share of Apple, but if the price of Apple goes up to $1, what you've made is $1. To profit using shares of stock, say by swing trading, you need to own a lot of shares of stock. As we'll see in a minute price changes in the stock are magnified in the option. If Apple goes up to $1, the options trader is going to be a lot better off than the guy who only buys one share with his $200.

Options Prices Change in Big Ways

The price or value of an option is directly related to the share price of the stock. It's not a one-to-one relationship in most cases, however. We'll see what the exact value is, but for now, let's say a call option for Apple stock is going to move in such a way that for every dollar Apple gains and losses, the price of the option will move by $0.80. This is on a per-share basis – so for the option overall, a $1 move in the stock means an $80 move in the value of the option.

This cut both ways, so options trading is not for the faint of heart. It also requires discipline. If you are watching an option over the course of a single day, you might see it go up and down by $50 in value if there is a lot of volatility.

But the advantage is a small price increase in stock can be led to big profits very quickly. Suppose that you bought that Apple option for $125. If the price per share of Apple goes up to $0.40, then the price of the option would rise to $157. Had it gone up to $1, the option would rise in price to $205.

Remember that goes both ways, so a decline in price by 40 cents would drop a $125 option to $93. Option prices can move fast throughout the day, so you have to be keeping a close eye on it so you don't get wiped out and in order to take advantage of opportunities to sell for profits.

The amount that each option's price moves with respect to the price of the underlying stock is something that varies depending on the individual option. We will discuss how to figure out the possible price changes later.

Options Have a Higher ROI

The return on investment for an option is much higher than for stocks. Let's say you had $5,000 to invest, and we used that to buy Apple shares at $200 a share. That would give us 25 shares. So, if the price went up by $2, that would give us a $50 profit, ignoring commissions. So, we'd have an ROI of:

ROI = \$50/\$5,000 x 100 = 1%

That really isn't a bad share increase for a single day move, investors in stocks are looking for a return of maybe 8% *per year.*

We could buy 40 options contracts at \$125 each. Using the preceding example where a \$1 move in the stock increases the per-share price of the option by \$0.80 a \$2 price increase would raise the price of the option from \$125 to \$285. The total profit per option contract is \$160. Our net profit with \$0 commissions on Robinhood would be \$6,400. The ROI in the options' case is:

ROI = \$6,400/\$5,000 x 100 = 128%

There are even bigger opportunities than this, on certain days you'll see stocks make big moves, like after an earnings announcement. The share price could go up to \$10 or \$20 if earnings beat expectations. The opportunities for profits are enormous.

Options Are Flexible

It's common to talk about call options because the concept is easier for beginners to understand, but put options give the options trader advantages a stock investor doesn't have. What if instead, the stock price of Apple dropped \$2? In that case, the investor in the Apple stock would lose \$50 instead. It's not a huge loss to be sure, but a loss is a loss.

But a clever options trader who saw the decline coming could have bought put options with their money. For the sake of simplicity, assuming that the price of the option was the same and it related to the stock price in the same way, the price of the put options would go up by $6,400 when the price of Apple dropped $2.

And we'll see later that you can devise strategies that will earn profits no matter which way the stock price moves. These techniques go by the name of the straddle, strangle, and iron condor among others.

Options Are Fast

Options have an expiration date. Some people will see this as a negative, but others will find it refreshing. Since options have an expiration date, they are not assets that you're going to hold onto very long (except for LEAPS). For those that like an asset with an expiration date, the result of this on a practical level is that with options you are going to get in and get out of your trades pretty quickly. You might periodically do day trades when a stock is experiencing large price movements. I typically do 2-3 a week (remember don't do 4 a week, unless you plan to deposit $25,000 and accept the day trader designation). In most cases, you'll hold the option for a couple of days and then sell it when the opportunity arises. If you are selling to open, then you'll be holding the position for anywhere from a week to a month or two. But there is no long-term investing.

CHAPTER 3:

The Basics of Options Trading and What It Is

What is Options Trading?

O ption contracts usually refer to the purchase or sale of certain assets. An option is a contract between two parties (a buyer and a seller), in which whoever buys the option acquires the right to exercise what the agreement indicates, although he will not have an obligation to do so.

Option contracts commonly refer to the purchase or sale of certain assets, which may be stocks, stock indices, bonds, or others. These contracts also establish that the operation must be carried out on a preestablished date (in the case of the European ones, since those of the US are exercised at any time) and at a fixed price at the time the contract is signed.

To purchase an option to buy or sell it is necessary to make an initial disbursement (called "premium,") whose value depends, fundamentally, on the price that the asset that is the object of the contract has on the market, on the variability of that price and of the period between the date on which the contract is signed and the date on which it expires.

Call and Put

The options that grant the right to buy are called 'Call,' and those that allow the right to sell is called 'Put.' Additionally, it is called European options that can only be exercised on the date of exercise and American Options that can be used at any time during the life of the contract.

When the time comes for the buying party to exercise the option, if it does, two situations occur:

- Whoever appears as the seller of the option will be obliged to do what they said contract indicates; that is, sell or buy the asset to the counterparty, in case it decides to exercise its right to buy or sell.

- Who appears as the option buyer will have the right to buy or sell the asset? However, if it doesn't suit you, you can refrain from making the transaction.

An option contract usually contains the following specifications:

- Exercise date: the expiration date of the right is included in the option.

- Exercise price: agreed price for the purchase/sale of the asset referred to in the contract (called an underlying asset).

- Option premium or price: amount paid to the counterparty to acquire the right to buy or sell.

- Rights acquired with the purchase of an option: they can be Call (right of purchase) and Put (right of sale).

- Types of Option: there may be Europeans, which are only exercised on the date of exercise or American, to be used at any time during the contract. There are, besides, other more complex types of options, the so-called "Exotic Options."

In international financial markets, the types of options that are traded on organized exchanges are typically American and European.

Practical Example

Purchase of a call option by an importing company to secure the Euro price on that day.

To better understand the use of options, this example is presented by an importing company that wants to ensure against increases in the price of the Euro.

To do so, you can buy a European call option today that gives you the right to buy a million euros, within three months, at $ 550 per euro. To acquire that right, the company pays $ 2 per euro, that is, the option premium has a cost of $ 2,000,000.

If on the expiration date of the option, the price of the euro in the market is over $ 550 (for example, at $ 560), the company will exercise the option to buy them, as it will only pay $ 550 per euro.

On the contrary, if on that date the market price of the Euro was below $ 550 (for example at $ 530), the company will not exercise the option, since it makes no sense to pay $ 550 per euro when it can be purchased at the market at $ 530; In this case, the option expires without being exercised.

The cash flows are as follows:

- Today (April 10, 20XX).

  Buy a European call option, which gives you the right to buy USD 1,000,000 to $ 550 on October 10, 20XX, as the value of the premium is 2 and 1,000,000 contracts are purchased (which means that the notional of the agreement is the US $ 1) there is a cash outlay of $ 2,000,000 for that concept.

- Expiration date (October 30, 20XX)

  If the Euro is above the exercise price of the option, it would be exercised, and $ 550 per euro will be paid, that is, $ 550,000,000.

  Otherwise, the option expires if it is used, and the euros are acquired in the market.

The euros purchased are used to cancel the importation of goods or services:

The following table shows the result of the operation. As can be seen, if on the expiration date of the option contract, the market exchange rate is lower than the exercise price of the call option, the importer will end up paying the market price per euro plus the cost of the premium (in strict rigor, the value of the premium should be updated for the interest that would have been earned if, instead of paying the value of the premium, that money had been deposited); otherwise, the cost of each euro will be equal to the exercise price plus the premium. That is, the importer will have made sure to pay a maximum of $ 552 per euro.

Market exchange rate A	The exercise price of the option B	Prima C	Value of the options (1) D = (A - B)	Result of the options (2) E = D - C	Disbursement for purchase of euros (3) F	Total disbursement G = F + C
530	550	2,000,0 00	0	- 2,000,00 0	530,000,000	532,000,000
540	550	2,000,0 00	0	- 2,000,00 0	540,000,000	542,000,000

550	550	2,000,0 00	0	- 2,000,00 0	550,000,000	552,000,000
560	550	2,000,0 00	10,000,0 00	8,000,00 0	550,000,000	552,000,000
570	550	2,000,0 00	20,000,0 00	18,000,0 00	550,000,000	552,000,000
580	550	2,000,0 00	30,000,0 00	28,000,0 00	550,000,000	552,000,000

Notes:

1. On the expiration date, when the price of the euro in the market is lower than the exercise price, the value of the call option will be zero (as it is not appropriate to exercise the purchase right), whereas, if the opposite occurs, the value of the call option will correspond to the difference between those two prices.
2. That result represents how much money was paid or saved by the fact of coverage.
3. Currencies are acquired in the market when it is not optimal to exercise the option, or by exercising the right of purchase when exercising that right is an optimal decision.

Finally, it should be noted that if a forward-type contract with the same delivery price had been used to perform the same coverage, the importer would have ended up always paying $ 550.

However, it would not have had the opportunities (which may appear when hedging with call options) to benefit from declines in the market exchange rate. Also, note that the operation is much simpler to perform: a premium is paid at the time of purchasing the option and on the expiration date (or at any time before that date if the option were of the American type) at least the price that has been agreed.

How the Options Work

Option operators must understand the complexity that surrounds them. The knowledge of the operation of the options allows operators to make the right decisions and offers them more options when executing a transaction.

Indicators:

- The value of an option consists of several elements that go hand in hand with the "Greeks"
- The price of the guaranteed value
- Expiration
- Implied volatility
- The actual exercise prices
- Dividends
- Interest rates

The "Greeks" provide valuable information on risk management and help rebalance the portfolios to achieve the desired exposure (e.g., delta coverage).

Each Greek measures the reaction of the portfolios to small changes in an underlying factor, which allows the individual risks to be examined:

- The delta measures the rate of change of the value of an option regarding changes in the price of the underlying asset.

- The gamma measures the rate of change in the delta with the changes suffered by the price of the underlying asset.

- Lambda or elasticity refers to the percentage change in the value of an option compared to the percentage change in the price of the underlying asset, which offers a method of calculating leverage, also known as "indebtedness."

- Theta calculates the sensitivity of the option value over time, a factor known as "temporary wear."

- Vega measures the susceptibility of the option of volatility. Vega measures the value of the option based on the volatility of the underlying asset.

- Rho represents the sensitivity of the value of an option against variations in the interest rate and measures the value of the option based on the risk-free interest rate.

Therefore, the Greeks are reasonably simple to determine if the Black Scholes model (considered the standard option valuation model) is used and is very useful for intraday and derivatives traders.

Delta, theta, and Vega are useful tools to measure time, price, and volatility.

The value of the option is directly affected by maturity and volatility if:

- For a long period before expiration, the value of the purchase and sale option tends to rise. The opposite situation would occur if, for a short period before expiration, the value of the purchase and sale options is prone to a fall.

- If the volatility increases, so will the value of the purchase and sale options, while if the volatility decreases, the value of the purchase and sale options decreases.

- The price of the guaranteed value causes a different effect on the value of the purchase options than on that of the sale options.

- Usually, as the price of the securities increases, so do the current purchase options that correspond to it, increasing its value while the sale options lose value?

- If the price of the value falls, the opposite happens, and the current purchase options usually experience a drop in value while the value of the sale options increases.

CHAPTER 4:

How to Start with Options Trading

W alking you through the learning curve of options trading will always start with the most basic move you'll need to make — setting yourself up in a position to actually be able to trade.

To trade-in options, you're going to need an options account. For now, it's important that you know your starting point and just how easy it is to reach it.

One thing to know before you pick your firm is that times have changed considerably over the last couple of decades when it comes to options trading. Back before the internet became such a constant part of our lives, your brokerage firm — or, at least, your representative at the firm—would make your options trades on your behalf and you paid a hefty price for their services. Nowadays, however, you'll be doing most of your trades yourself.

Commissions for your representative is, thus, a whole lot lower than it used to be which means it won't cost you an arm and both legs to rely on your rep in the early days of your experience with options. While you are learning, feel free to make use of your firm's services to place and confirm your trades if it helps you to feel more comfortable getting to know the process.

With that in mind, there are going to be certain things to look for when you select your firm.

- Compare commission prices to make sure you're getting a great deal.

- Make sure the firm has up-to-date software and is capable of setting up trades quickly and reliably to make sure you get the trades you want at the best prices.

- Check out the hours of service to ensure the firm is compatible with your needs. In these days of online firms, you could be dealing with a firm that's across the ocean from the markets you have an interest in. Or you might find that a firm only makes its reps available for the length of the working day and that might not suit your own timing.

- Speak personally with the reps at the firm because these are the people who are going to help you during the process of setting up your strategy. You want someone who is personable and knowledgeable—and, most importantly, who speaks in terms that you personally find easy to comprehend.

- Take a look at the additional services the firm supplies. Many will offer learning materials, guides, and even classes or webinars to help you hone your strategies. Even if you feel that you already know what you need to know, there's no harm in a refresher course or a little nugget of inspiration every once in a while.

Once you select a firm, you'll then need to consider signing a "margin agreement" with that firm. That agreement allows you to borrow money from the firm in order to purchase your stocks, which is known as "buying on margin."

Understandably, your brokerage firm is not going to allow you to buy on margin if you don't have the financial status to pay them back. They will, therefore, run a credit check on you and ask you for information about your resources and your knowledge.

A margin account is not a necessity for options trading — you don't actually use margin to purchase an option because it must be paid for in full. However, a margin account can be useful as you graduate to more advanced strategies and, in some cases, it will be obligatory. If you opt to sign a margin agreement, talk it through thoroughly with the firm as there are certain restrictions on the type of money you can use that may apply to you.

Next, you'll need to sign an "options agreement." This time, it's an obligatory step. That agreement is designed to figure out how much you know about options and how much experience you have with trading them. It also aims to ensure that you are absolutely aware of the risks you take by trading options and it is to make sure that you are financially able to handle those risks.

By ascertaining those things, your firm can determine what level of options trading you should be aiming for. It will, therefore, approve your "trading level" and there are five levels.

- Level 1: You may sell covered calls.
- Level 2: You may buy calls and puts and also buy strangles, straddles, and collars. You may also sell puts that are covered by cash and by options on exchange-traded funds and indexes.
- Level 3: You may utilize credit and debit spreads.
- Level 4: You may sell "naked puts," straddles, and strangles.
- Level 5: You may sell "naked indexes" and "index spreads."

Don't worry if you're not sure yet what each of those things means. You will understand them by the time you finish reading this book. For now, all you need to be aware of is that your firm will determine what level is appropriate for you. As a beginner, don't be surprised if you only reach the first two levels.

Once you've signed the option agreement, you'll be handed a booklet that contains a mine of information about the risks and rewards within options trading. Right now, if you were to read that booklet, it would seem to be in a foreign language. By the time you finish this crash course, it will be a lot more understandable — and it's very important for your success that you do read it.

Finally, your firm will present you with a "standardized option contract." It's the same for every trader, which means you stand the same chance of success as every other person out there in the options market.

By trading an option, you are entering into a legal agreement that is insured by the Options Clearing Corporation, which guarantees the contract will be honored in full. Make sure you read that contract to be aware of not only the rights you have as a trader but also the obligations you must follow in the same role.

Congratulations, you now have an options account. That is the conduit through which you will create and implement your strategies and begin your adventure in options trading.

CHAPTER 5:

The Most Important Types of Options Trading

T here are generally two major classes of options. These are put options and call options.

Put options give you, the investor, and an opportunity to sell stocks at a specified price while call options give you the option to buy stocks at a certain price.

Underlying Asset

Every option contract is based on an underlying asset. Most options are based on stocks of companies that are listed in the stock market. In recent years though, other securities have been used.

These include REITs or real estate investment trusts, ETFs, or electronically traded funds, foreign currencies, and stock indices. Some are even based on commodities like minerals, industrial, and agricultural products.

Stock options contracts are generally based on 100 shares of the underlying stock.

Some exceptions are made in special cases for instance where mergers occur or when there is a stock split.

Also, buying options is completely different from investing in shares. Here is a look at different types of options.

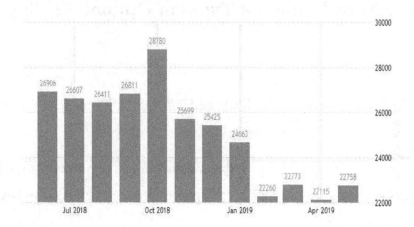

Different Types of Options

Near Month in-the-Money Options

Some options are best suited for day trading. One such example is the near-month-in-the-month option. This option refers to options contracts that are set to expire at the close of the next month. Such options are usually past their strike price, so investors are free to exercise them.

The inherent value of this option's contract is one of the determining factors of the premium especially when it nears its expiration date. Such options are often traded in large volumes and this causes a smaller gap between the asking and bidding prices. As the option nears its expiration date, its time value diminishes.

Protective Put Option

A protective put is an option that is used by traders who wish to purchase both an option and its underlying securities. This is the preferred strategy anytime that the underlying stock is expected to undergo periods of high volatility.

There are instances when day traders will continually buy and sell the same stock option for a long time, maybe a couple of months, to benefit from a short-term upward trend. At other times, day traders make use of a strategy of purchasing put options on the same underlying security just so they insure themselves against any sharp losses in the stock's price. This is considered a risk management technique. While there are certain small losses paid to protect the share, the opportunity to minimize losses on a downward trend is invaluable.

Stock Options

Traders acquire a way to increase their profits through straightforward stock options by simply purchasing or shorting shares at a certain set price at a set date at the options market. Day traders have certain advantages when it comes to stock options because the parameters are applied to stock options. Since both stock options and stocks are traded on an exchange, the market will have the same liquidity and will enable the fast execution of orders. Sophisticated investors can use options as an effective hedge against risks.

Stock options have the potential to cost you 100% of your funds. Brokers only permit sophisticated traders to deal in complex options systems like stock options. You can be exposed to enormous amounts of risk and you must avoid strategies that require substantial experience. But it is good to note that day traders rarely sell options.

Weekly Options

Weekly options are also popularly referred to as weeklies. Such options are generally listed with only one week left to expiration. Most options often have several months and sometimes even years to expiration. However, weeklies are generally available to day traders. They are found on ETNs or exchange-traded notes, broad-market indices in the US, and ETFs or exchange-traded funds. A lot of traders view traditional options as a huge setback largely because of the long-time duration. These traders very much prefer weeklies and view them as major game-changers. They get to apply the leverage of options even as they engage in more short-term strategies.

Created on Thursdays

Weekly contracts are usually created once each week on a Thursday. They remain valid until the following Friday for ETNs, ETFs, and equities. Weekly index options, however, often close their final trading sessions on Fridays or Thursdays depending on the index. These have a total lifetime of seven trading days or one week. As a day trader, you can benefit hugely if you take advantage of the increased volatility that comes with the time decay and expiration that is associated with options. Weekly options have 52 expiration periods throughout the year and this increases your chances of benefiting from expiring options. While weeklies provide a couple of advantages to day traders, they have some possible disadvantages especially due to time factors. Option buyers generally pay a lower price for the cost of a weekly option compared to regular options. They usually experience a hugely limited opportunity window, especially when trades move in the opposite of the intended direction. There is generally a very limited opportunity for the price to recover and it is hard to fix a trade through strike adjustments.

Mini Options

Mini options are options that let traders and investor's trade-in options that are based on 10-share sets rather than the standard 100-share sets. Mini options have expiration dates that are similar to regular expiration dates. This expiration date is also similar to quarterlies and weeklies.

Other features like the bids, strike price, and offers are also similar and correspond to features of regular options. However, they do offer certain benefits. As a trader, you stand to enjoy the following benefits by simply trading in mini options.

Index Options

We also have another type of options contract which is known as the index option. These options let you make use of put or call options to speculate on the movements of a whole stock market index like the S&P 500 or the Dow Jones instead of individual stocks and shares. A trader who trades index options can capitalize on their predictions based on volatility or direction of an entire market without any need to trade options based on individual stocks. One of the main challenges that traders encounter when pricing index options is accurately calculating dividend estimates.

Binary Options

Binary options are among the most commonly traded options. They are known by different names depending on the platform where they are trading. For instance, binary options are referred to as FROs or fixed return options when traded on the American Stock Exchange. On the Forex markets, they are referred to as digital options and sometimes as all-or-nothing options on the ASE or American Stock Exchange. The reason why they are known as binary is that this options class offers returns or profits in two outcomes. This means you get something or nothing. In this instance where you have binary options, the profitability is usually a pre-set amount such as $100. Certain assets can be traded as binary options. These assets include:

- Stocks
- Commodities
- Currencies
- Stock indices
- While there are plenty of different binary options types, only two are commonly used by day traders. These popular binary options are:
  - o Cash or nothing binary options
  - o Asset or nothing binary options

The reasoning behind binary options day trading is pretty simple. As a trader, the aim is to enter a trade position and exit before the close of the trading day. All binary options contracts come with expiry times and dates. This means that most binary options contracts have a set expiry date except on trading platforms where traders have variable expiry on options. As a day trader, you should identify expiry dates that will conclude trades within the same day. This is because once you enter a trade that has an expiry date, you will not be able to exit manually the same way that you do with all other options trades.

Futures Options

Options on futures are contracts that are focused on one futures contract. As a buyer, you reserve the right to choose a futures position on an index, currency, commodity, or other financial prices. The options trade is at a specified price known as the strike price and you maintain your right until the expiration of the option. A future options seller is obligated by the contract to assume the reverse futures position as soon as you exercise your right. These options trades are dealt with on the same exchanges with traditional futures contracts. The options contracts concisely match the underlying securities, which in this case are futures contracts. The matching is in terms of the strike price, expiration dates, and quantities.

There are certain differences between futures and options futures. As an example, buyers and sellers have different obligations. It is advisable to find out more about the differences between options on futures contracts and futures contracts.

ETF Options

An ETF option is an options contract that is derived from the ETF or exchange-traded fund. ETFs are investment pools that are then traded at the stock market. Electronically traded funds contain a specific number of underlying assets that include bonds, commodities, and stocks. They trade very near to the net asset value throughout the trading day.

The shares and other financial instruments are traded in much the same manner as for regular stocks at the bourse. This way, a trader is easily able to purchase and sell shares and even options of an electronically traded fund via a brokerage account. You will find ETFs across all the common stock indexes such as the Nasdaq 100 composite (QQQQ) and the Dow Jones Industrial Average. Sometimes traders will choose a specific industry because chances are high of finding stocks of major industries across most ETFs. This way, traders can focus more on determining and predicting movements in a specific industry rather than a mixed choice of stocks as offered by standard index ETFs.

ETF options come in very handy as their related options trade throughout the day. As a day trader, if you actively trade ETF options and make use of hedging strategies, then you need to ensure that you are well informed regarding the background information of the underlying stock. If you feel confident about this information, then you will gain from the tax breaks and low costs associated with trading ETF options.

IRA or Individual Retirement Accounts Options

Yet another option account that is out there is the IRA options contract. However, IRA accounts are generally unavailable to the general population because of rules put in place by the SEC or US Securities and Exchange Commission.

The SEC demands that any day trader have the appropriate designation and should hold margin brokerage accounts. However, this is not the case when it comes to an IRA account. Such accounts cannot be margin accounts and are limited to only cash accounts.

In simple terms, day trading of stock options and stocks needs traders to operate a margin account and any IRA account used should have only a cash account status. The only alternative that you can have is to create your own IRA account via a commodity futures broker.

CHAPTER 6:

Strategies and Tips for Options Trading

Tips for Option Trading

L et me stop you right there before you start making trades. There are a few things you need to be aware of before you enter the market; here are the steps you need to go through.

1. Portfolio Balance

Before you do anything, you need to look at your portfolio balance first. When you're planning a new trade, it's always important to ask yourself why you need that trade and how it will affect your portfolio. Do you even really need it? For instance, if your portfolio already has plenty of bearish trades, it would generally be better for you to avoid adding more.

You need to reduce your risk in every situation, so the key here is to balance out your trades. That's how one develops a great portfolio, risk diversification. When you have a bunch of bearish trades in hand, look for bullish trades to offset the risk and vice versa. Once you internalize this, it becomes far easier to focus on what your portfolio really needs and filter out the rest from the very first moment you start looking for a new trade.

2. Liquidity

Liquidity is straight-up one of the most important qualities of a good, tradable option. You don't want to be stuck with an illiquid option, no matter how lucrative it looks. Here's a simple rule to follow when looking for a new trade: for it to be a good trade, the underlying stock should be trading at least 100,000 shares daily. If the numbers are less than that, the trade isn't worth your time. In a market as big and efficient as the one we have, the calculations only become more accurate with the passage of time. Similarly, when considering the underlying options, there should be a minimum of 1000 open interest contracts for the strikes you are trading for it to be a good trade.

3. **Implied Volatility Percentile**

Say, if AAPL has an IV of 35%, but an IV percentile of 70%, it means that while the current volatility is low, in the last year, it was higher than what it currently is (35%) for more than 70% of the time. So, the implied volatility for AAPL is relatively high, and you should be looking to employ premium-selling strategies.

4. **Picking a Strategy**

Picking a great strategy is as much a matter of eliminating as it is a matter of selecting, perhaps even more so. You can easily eliminate a bunch of strategies once you have a good idea of the IV and the IV percentile of the underlying stock and how it affects the options. For example, it's easy to eliminate strategies like debit spreads and long single options when you know the IV is high and the pricing rich. Then it's time to consider our risk tolerance and account size to pick the best strategy out of the ones left (iron condors, credit spreads, strangles, etc.)

5. **Strikes & Month**

Your personal trading style and goals also play a big part in how you decide to pick trades. Some people are more risk-averse than others, and that's okay. You should always select the right strategy based on the risk level you're comfortable with. If you're selling credit spreads, let's say, and you have the option to sell them at a strike price that has a 90% chance of success a strike price has a 65% chance of success, you need to decide which option you want to go with based on the level of aggression you're comfortable with. It needs to fit your trading style and your goals.

6. Future Moves

You must've heard the popular saying that a chess grandmaster can foresee as many as 20 moves ahead. A good options trader also plans ahead and foresees future moves. If you're not thinking a few moves ahead, you're going to lose to the market more often than not. Always have a Plan B in case things go nasty and you need to shield yourself from losses.

Sometimes, you just won't be able to make a winning trade. That's just how the market works; some trades go wrong no matter how well you plan. But you need to keep asking yourself important questions constantly. When you do this, your mind stays sharp and ready to jump into action to formulate a new plan or make an adjustment as and when the need arises.

Trading Strategies

When all is said in done, you are the one responsible for turning your venture into foreign exchange into a successful endeavor. That is actually one of the great things about the stock. You do not have a boss screaming down your neck, telling you to do something that you do not agree with.

You have the ability to come up with your own trading plan based on your own research and your own knowledge. That being said, success can come more quickly for some than for others, and a lot of the time, this has to do with approaching this endeavor with the right strategy.

Strategy 1. Buy Low and Sell High

If you began stock trading today with $25,000 in your pocket and access to a trading platform, all ready and raring to go, how would you know what is low and what is high? It's your first day. Naturally, for you to understand what would represent a good low investment and conversely what is high, you need to have some knowledge of the exchange rate history of that currency. Maybe the exchange rate for the Japanese yen seems low, but actually, compared to last year or a few months ago, it's a little high. Now it would not be a good time to buy. Maybe the pound seems low right now, but yesterday the British government announced that the first round of the Brexit negotiations with the EU failed, and, therefore, the pound may have room to go lower than it was when you logged onto your trading platform. Maybe you should wait and see what the pound is later today or tomorrow and buy then. The point here is that buying low and selling high requires understanding the patterns associated with that stock and what might cause it to go up or down. And that's merely the buying side of things. A good plan will prevent you from selling too soon, or even not selling soon enough.

Strategy 2. Focus on Not Losing Money Rather Than on Making Money

This may not be an easy strategy to understand initially, in part because not losing money and making money seem like two sides of the same coin. They are, but they are not identical. One of the personality types that is associated with difficulty in finding success in trading is the impulsive type. This type of person wants to make money, and they want to make it quick. They have a vague strategy about how they plan on doing that, but the most important thing to them is that they have a high account balance to make as many trades as they need to turn a profit. This is the wrong approach. Currencies are not the same as stocks. The value of a stock may change very little even after a week's time, so my strategy involves a lot of trades in order to make money is usually not the best strategy.

Strategy 3. Develop a Sense of Sentiment Analysis

Alright, the third strategy was going to be about Fibonacci retracement, which is a type of technical analysis of the market, but as this is the basics of stock trading, we are going to go into a different strategy that is not any easier than a Fibonacci retracement, just different. Sentiment analysis is a term that is used in many different specialties, not just finance, and it is not easy to describe. A key to understanding sentiment analysis is likening it to public opinion.

The economy may be booming, people have more money in their pocket, so the stock of this hypothetical country should increase in value, but maybe it doesn't. Maybe there is something that is causing the market to be bearish and which, therefore, might cause the stock to drop.

As you perhaps can tell, as this analysis is not based on any concrete information, it can be thought of as intuitive, and no one has intuition on day 1. Let's just be honest about that. Intuition comes from experience. But the purpose of this strategy is to introduce to you the idea that not the foreign exchange market, like any market, is not going to behave like a machine because it's not a machine. Markets are places where human beings come together, and humans are unpredictable, often in a frustrating way.

Research

Regardless of the investment that you make, be sure always to do your research. Doing research is a must. It is what will increase your chances of making the right investment decision. As the saying goes, "Knowledge is power." The more that you understand something, the more likely it that you will be able to predict how it will move in the market. This is why doing research is essential. It will allow you to know if something is worth investing in or not. Remember that you are dealing with a continuously moving market, so it is only right that you keep yourself updated with the latest developments and changes, and the way to do this is by doing research.

Remember that gaining information is not limited to just surfing the web for information. It is also suggested that you join online groups and forums that are related to your chosen investment. There is also a good chance that you can learn something from them.

Do not rush the process of doing research. Take note that you make decisions based on the information that you have on hand, and such information that you have will depend on the time and efforts that you put into doing research. Make sure that all of your decisions are backed up by solid research and analysis.

Have a Plan

Whether you are going to start forex trading or trade in general, it is always good to have a plan. Make sure to set a clear direction for yourself. This is also an excellent way to avoid being controlled by your emotions or becoming greedy. You should have a short-term plan and a long-term plan. Poor planning leads to poor execution, but having a good idea usually ends up favorably. You should stick to your plan. However, there are certain instances when you may have to abandon your project, such as when you realize that sticking to the same program will not lead to a desirable outcome or in case you find a much better idea. Proper planning can give you a sense of direction and ensure the success of execution.

Make your plans practical and reasonable. Remember that you ought to stick to whatever project you come up with, so be sure to keep your ideas real. Before you come up with an idea, you must first have quality information. Again, this is why doing research is very important.

CHAPTER 7:

Lingo Learning

E very industry has its own specialized lingo, and options trading is no exception. Let's give a quick overview that will help you understand what is being deliberated when reading about options and help you navigate the markets effectively.

Ask

The price that a seller is asking for security or put another way the smallest price a seller is willing to accept to sell it.

Assignment

When the buyer of an options contract exercises their option, a notice is sent to the seller. The seller is then obligated to dispose of (in the case of a call) or purchase (in the case of a put) stocks at the strike price.

At the Money

This means that the current market price is equal to the strike price.

Bid Price

This term refers to the optimum amount that a dealer is willing to shell out for security.

Break-Even Point

When neither a profit nor loss has been realized.

Call

The buyer of a call option has the right to buy 100 shares of a stock at the strike price at any time before the options contract expires. This is an option, so the buyer does not have to buy the shares. The seller of a call contract must buy the shares under any circumstances up to the expiration of the contract if the buyer exercises their right before the contract expires.

Commission

A fee is charged by a brokerage firm to execute an option order on an exchange.

Delta

If the underlying stock changes by a point in value, the delta is the change in the value of the option.

Early Exercise

If an options contract is exercised before the expiration date, it is said to be early.

Exercise

The buyer of the option exercises their right to buy stock for a call or sell the stock for a put.

Expiration Date

Options contracts expire on the third Friday of every month. When you see an option quote such as:

- JUN 70

That means that the option expires on the third Friday in June, with a strike price of $70.

In the Money (Call)

This refers to the occurrence of when the current market price exceeds the strike price. This is the gross profit per share (not including premium and other fees).

In the Money (Put)

For a put contract, it is in-the-money when the current stock price is less than the strike price.

Index Options

An index option doesn't have individual stocks as the underlying. Instead, the underlying is an index like the NASDAQ. An index option can't be exercised until the expiry date.

Intrinsic Value

An apt example would be – if the current price is at $10, then the market price is at $20, the intrinsic value would be $10. If the current price were $25, the intrinsic value would be $15.

LEAP

A LEAP is a long-term equity anticipation security. Basically, these are long term options contracts. LEAP contracts can last as long as three years. LEAPS are generally more expensive than most options, because of the longtime value which gives them more time to be "in the money."

Legs

A leg is one part of a position when there are two or more options or positions in the underlying stock.

Long

Long means ownership when it is held in your account. You can belong on a stock or an option.

Margin Requirement

If you are selling options, you will be required to deposit some cash with the brokerage to cover your positions. In other words, it is cash in your account with the brokerage to buy or sell shares as required by your obligations in the options contract.

Option Chain

An option chain is something you'll look at when viewing available options online. It's basically a table for the options available for a given underlying stock. For a given expiration date, the option chain will include all puts and calls, and strike prices that are available.

Out-of-the-Money

This is the amount that a stock price is lower the strike price for a call, or overhead the strike price for a put. If your price $50 but the market is $40, you're "out of the money" $10. If your strike price for a put is $50, but the market price is $60, you're out of the money $10.

Premium

This is the price paid per share for an options contract.

Since the contract has 100 shares, the price paid, or the total premium is 100 times the premium.

The seller is able to keep the premium regardless of whether or not the buyer exercises their options.

Put

The buyer of a put option has the rightful authority to trade 100 shares at the strike price on or before the expiry date.

The seller of a put option has a responsibility to buy 100 shares if required by the buyer.

Roll a Long Position

Rolling a long position means to sell options and then acquire others with the same underlying stock but with different strike prices and expiration dates.

Roll a Short Position

Rolling a short position means buying to close an existing position and selling for the purposes of opening new positions with different strike prices and expiration dates "rolled out" in time.

Series

Options are grouped together in series on the markets.

Options in the same series can be calls or puts, but they have the same expiration date and strike price.

Short

Selling a security that you don't actually own.

Strike Price

It is the amount per share of the agreed-upon contract. If the option to buy or sell is exercised by the purchaser of an options contract, the shares must be bought or sold at the strike price.

When you look at options online, the strike price is given at the end of the options symbol.

For example, you might see:

- 00040000

  The decimal point is found by moving three places from the right. So, this represents a strike price of $40. Alternatively

- 00005600

  It would represent a strike price of $5.60.

Time Value

How long is left until an options contract expires? Generally, more time value will mean that an option is worth more when trading. The reason is that the more time until the option expires, the more chance there is for the underlying stock to beat the strike price. In the case of a call option that means going above the strike price, while in the case of a put option that means going below the strike price. What investors are looking for is enough time value for an option to be in the money.

Time Decay

Time decay is simply a measure of the decrease in the time value of an options contract.

Underlying

The underlying stock is the specific stock that the option contract is based on. This is the stock that is actually traded if the option is exercised.

Weekly

A weekly is a kind of option that expires within a week, rather than a monthly time frame. Since weekly's have a short time value, they are cheaper, but the risks involved are higher. Investors who like weeklies are hoping to capitalize on an option that tightly fits a given date coming up in the near future.

Weekly's usually expired on Friday afternoons at market close. Weeklies help traders that are trying to exploit short term events for profits. For example, investors might target an earnings report or an anticipated product announcement.

CHAPTER 8:

Covered Call Strategies, Examples

W e are going to look at the two most conservative strategies. The strategies are not going to be available for everyone, but these are the strategies that are allowed for a level one trader. The reason that they're allowed for level one trader is that these types of options are backed with collateral. In order to use the strategies, you must either have the asset on hand, or in the case of a put option, you must have money in your account to completely cover the purchase of shares should it come to that.

The main purpose of the strategies is to generate a monthly income. If you already own many shares of one particular stock, this can be an appealing way to earn income off the stock.

Covered Calls

The first strategy that we are going to consider is known as a covered call. When you write a covered call, you are selling an option against shares of stock that you already own. In order to sell one options contract, you have to cover it with your own shares of stock. And you must have 100 for each contract. In return for writing the options contract and selling to open, you will receive a premium payment that you are allowed to keep no matter what happens.

When selling covered call, chances are you're going to want to keep the shares of stock. Selling an in the money call option is probably not going to be something that you will risk doing. A word of caution is in order here. If you look online, you're going to see article after article which will tell you that 85% of options expire as worthless. This statistic gives a very false impression. Those options that expire as worthless were probably out of the money. If you sell a call option and it expires in the money, you are going to be assigned. What this means in the case of a call option, is that you will be required to sell the underlying shares of stock. Since you have invested in the stock, and you're trying to make a monthly income off the shares, chances are you want to avoid selling the shares. You are more likely going to be interested in selling and out of the money option on the shares.

Examples

Let's have a look at some examples so that we can get an idea of how much money could be generated. For our first example, I'm going to be a bit optimistic and assume that you own 100 shares of Amazon. If you do, that could be a pretty good deal because the options are expensive. In our example, 1 share of stock is priced at $53.85. If we sold one call option, we could get a monthly income of $5385, which is the premium that will be required to purchase this option. This option is out of the money. But consider examining delta, so that we can get an idea of the risk involved in selling a covered call that has a strike price as given. Delta is given at 0.4563. This means that there is a 46% chance that this option will expire in the money. The breakeven price is $2053.85. The breakeven price of an option is something you need to pay attention to when you're selling to open. This will give you an idea of the actual share price that will be required in order for someone to exercise the option. That gives us a little room, as long as Amazon doesn't move too much over the time period before the expiration of this option. When selling options, oftentimes, you want to take advantage of the time decay. Time decay is our friend if we are selling to open an options contract. Let's consider an alternative, and look at some options that are about to expire. At the time of writing, the share price of Amazon's $1971.90. Consequently, a $200 call that expires in three days is currently selling at $36.85. In theory, you could make around $3600 within one week by selling a call option on your Amazon shares. But remember that there is always the risk of assignment if the option expires in the money. This is where Bollinger bands can come in handy.

You can look to see what the one standard deviation price levels are, and then you can sell options that are at least one standard deviation away from the current share price. This reduces your risk significantly since there is a 68% probability that the market value is going to state within one standard deviation of the current price. Also, with time decay working in our favor, selling an option with just a few days left before expiration is a pretty safe move most of the time. Of course, Amazon is an extreme example because of the very high share price. Let's take a look at something that has a more reasonable price like Facebook. It's currently trading at $199 a share. The prices of Facebook are actually pretty high right now and the reason is there is an upcoming earnings call. But we can look at the chance of profit when choosing a call option that we can use to sell to open. Your broker will estimate the chance of profit for selling an option. Under normal circumstances, I would be willing to sell it $205 call that expired in two weeks. Under the current circumstances, I probably wouldn't do it because the earnings call might send this share price skyrocketing. In any case, there's a 72.4% chance of profit with the $205 dollar call and the price for the call option is $5.95. For every 100-share option that we sold, we will earn $595 in premium. This is actually a pretty nice income as well. And of course, the more shares you own, the more money you can make. If you own 1000 shares of Facebook, you could put a portion of your portfolio at risk, and you could still potentially earn a full time living selling covered calls.

Selling Options Strategy: Buy It Back

Now, we are going to talk about a defense mechanism that you can use to protect yourself when selling options. It doesn't matter what type of option or strategy that you're using. But we will introduce it in the case of covered calls.

Chances are even if you could make cold hard cash selling the shares at the strike price, you probably want to hold onto the shares. The first thing to realize is that if an option goes in the money, although it can't be exercised at any time, in most circumstances, it is not going to be exercised until it's very close to expiration or actually at the expiration. This fact gives option sellers a strategy they can use to protect themselves from being assigned. In the case of call options that would mean that you would be able to earn an income off of the shares, while at the same time getting some reasonable protection as far as being able to keep the shares.

This strategy relies on the time decay of options. If an option is out of the money, all the value of the option is extrinsic value. This implies that the option does not get direct value from the stock market price, although its price can fluctuate based on changes in the stock price. But the main thing about this is that when an option has 100% of its value locked up in extrinsic value, it is very sensitive to time decay. As the option approaches expiration, its value is going to decline rapidly. Remember that time decay is nonlinear. The closer you get to expiration, the faster it's going to drop.

To take advantage of this, you can actually buy back the option that you sold. It's not going to be the exact same option. You only have to buy back an option that has the same expiration date and strike price. Your broker probably has this set up for you anyway. In that case, you will probably be able to access a close button from your dashboard which will allow you to close the position by purchasing the option back. This is going to lower your profit somewhat. For some options, you might have sold it for $500, and then you have to buy it back for $150. Of course, this is not ideal because you're cutting into your profits. But you still walk away with the $350 premium.

If there is no risk going to the end of the expiration date that is to be exercised, then this strategy really isn't necessary. Some people are more conservative than others, and so they will use this strategy as a matter, of course. I have to admit that is a smart way to do it, even though you are cutting into the profits you could make. However, some people are willing to take that risk of just letting the options expire. That way, they get the full profit from the $500 premium. This can be a reasonable approach in the situation that there is no real chance that on the last day of the option contract the price is going to suddenly shift and put your option in the money. Therefore, this is going to have to be a situation that you would evaluate for each individual situation. It's also going to depend on the amount of risk that you are able to tolerate. But I just wanted to go through this process, so that readers could understand the way that you get out of having the option exercise on you.

Options that Expire in The Money Will be Exercised

Therefore, this is an important point to make because so much material out on the Internet makes it sound like there is little to no risk that an option is going to be exercised. Here are the facts. If an option expires in the money, the probability that it will be exercised is 100%. This is because the broker will exercise the option. If you are selling options, and they're in the money, you don't want to let them expire.

Strategy: Protected Puts

The next strategy that we are going to examine is called a protected put. A protected put is an analog to a covered call. In order to sell a protected, put, you must have enough capital in your account to cover a possible sale of the stock. This will be sold for the strike price used to sell the option. If you were to sell a $195 put on Facebook that expired in 17 days, you would need to have $19,500 in cash in your account, in case the option was exercised. You would receive a premium payment of $438. The premium is yours to keep, but a lot of people would be leery of tying up that much capital to make $438. Of course, to be fair you would need to compare that to putting the money in the bank or in bonds and seeing how much interest you would earn over 17 days. Selling a protective put is probably not the best strategy to use when trading options, but it is going to generate a lot more income than most other available means to do so in the present environment.

If you have the capital to cover the sale, this is not a bad move. The rule that is usually given is that you should be willing to own the stock. The price that you must be willing to pay would be the strike price. Think about this before selling a put option. In this example, walking away with 100 shares of Facebook is not a bad deal. You still end up with a solid asset in your portfolio. Of course, the option wouldn't be exercised unless Facebook stock had dropped significantly, making exercising the option possible and desirable. But over the long term, this is probably a good deal because the Facebook stock is going to appreciate it down the road.

Dividend Warning

One problem with selling options contracts is considering stocks that have dividends. If a stock pays a dividend, this could be an additional risk. Some traders will exercise an option to get the dividend payment. This still isn't going to happen unless the trader is going to profit from the deal, so you are going to be looking at options that are in the money. When selling covered calls on stocks that pay a dividend, you will want to avoid selling around the ex-dividend date. If the transfer of shares occurs with the buyer as the shareholder of record, you will miss out on the dividend payment.

CHAPTER 9:

Volatility

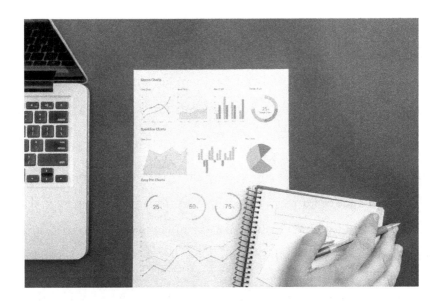

There's one final factor that affects the prices of contracts on a fundamental basis, though it's not something we've touched on so far. The volatility of a contract is, however, an incredibly important concept to grasp for an options trader.

What is Volatility?

Volatility refers to the movement of the underlying stock. Some stocks will slowly wend their way up and down in a predictable manner – those are not very volatile. Others charge on a day-to-day basis and change between up and down along the way.

To sum up the effect of volatility in a single sentence: the more volatile the stock, the more that an options trader is willing to pay for it. A volatile stock has a better chance of reaching the strike price and perhaps shooting far beyond it before the expiration date.

However, it's also the most dangerous of the factors that you need to bear in mind because it's arguably the most likely one to force you into a bad decision. A volatile stock, for example, can lead to a much higher premium and therefore a higher contract price; unless that stock shoots through the roof, you could end up losing money even when you should be making it.

One way to estimate the volatility of a stock is to take a look at what it has done in the recent past. This tells you how much it has moved up and down already, which some use as an indicator of how much it will move up and down in the future.

Unfortunately, it's not always true that the past repeats itself and you can't predict the future based on what's already happened. Instead, options traders use "implied volatility" to make their guesses: the value that the market believes the option is worth.

You can see this reflected in the activity on the options for that stock. Buyers will be keen to get their hands-on options before a certain event takes place, such as the announcement of a new product or a release about the company's earnings. Because of this, options increase in price because there is implied volatility – the market thinks the stock is going to shoot up.

You'll see lower demand on a stock that's flat or moving gently because there is no implied volatility and therefore no hurry to get in on the action. You'll also see correspondingly low prices for the option.

Volatility is a good thing – as a buyer, you want the stock to be volatile because you need it to climb to the strike price and beyond. However, there is also such a thing as too much volatility. It's at that point the contracts become popular, the prices rise, and you stand to pay more for a contract than you will ultimately profit.

Your brokers will likely be able to provide you with a program that will help you determine implied volatility, asking you to enter certain factors and then calculating it for you. However, it's only through experience that you'll learn how to spot a stock that's just volatile enough to justify its higher price – again, practice is key.

It's also worth noting that a lot of the risk in options trading comes from volatility, largely because it's impossible to be accurate in your estimates. What happens if an earthquake destroys that company's headquarters? Stocks are going to plummet, and you had absolutely no way to see it coming.

That's why options traders are forced to accept that their fancy formulas are not going to be perfect predictors. They will help, but you should still be conservative in your trading and avoid the temptation to sink everything into a trade you believe could make your fortune thanks to its volatility.

Strategies for a Volatile Market

Long Straddle

This strategy is essentially an amalgamation of the long call and long put trading strategies. You will be using the money options for executing the strategy. You are required to purchase at the money calls along with at the money puts of the same amount. Execute both these transactions simultaneously and ensure that the expiry date for them stays the same. Given that the expiry date is long-term, it gives the underlying security sufficient time to show a price movement and increases your chances of earning a profit. A short-term expiration date doesn't provide much scope for any changes in the price of an asset, so the profitability is also relatively low.

Long Strangle

This is also known as the strangle strategy, and you must place simultaneous orders with your broker. You must purchase calls on relevant security and then by the same number of puts on the security. The options contracts you execute must be out of the money and must be made simultaneously.

The best way to go about it is to purchase those securities that are just out of the money instead of ones that are far out of the money. Make sure that the strike prices in both these transactions are equidistant from the existing trading price of the underlying asset.

Strip Straddle

This strategy is quite similar to a long straddle- you will be purchasing at the money calls and the money puts. The only difference is that the number of puts you purchase will be higher than the calls your purchase. The expiry date and the underlying asset for both these transactions you make will be the same. The only factor upon which your profitability lies in the ratio of puts to calls you use. The best ratio is to purchase two puts for every call you make.

Strip Strangle

You stand to earn a profit if the underlying asset makes a big price movement in either direction is. However, your profitability increases if the price movement is downwards instead of upwards. You will be required to purchase out of the money calls and out of the money puts. Ensure that the number of the money puts you make are greater than the out of money calls you to decide to make. So, to begin with, the ratio of 2:1 will work well for you.

Strap Straddle

This is quite similar to the long straddle strategy- you are required to purchase at the money calls along with at the money puts for the same date of expiry. You are required to purchase more calls than ports, and the basic ratio to start with is 2:1. User strategy for certain that there will be an upward movement in the price of the underlying asset instead of a downward price movement.

Strap Strangle

This is quite similar to the Long strangle strategy and uses it when you're quite confident that there will be a dramatic movement in the price of the underlying strategy. You tend to earn a profit if the price moves in either direction, but your profitability increases in the price movement are upward. There are two transactions you must execute- purchase out of the money puts and purchase out of the money calls options. However, the number of out of the money calls you to make must be greater than the out of the money puts. The ratio of out of the money puts out of the money calls must be two to one. So, you will essentially be purchasing twice as many calls as sports.

Long Gut

You are required to purchase in the money call options along with an equal number of in the money put options. All of these will be based on the same underlying security along with the same date of expiration. The decisions you are required to make while using the strategy are related to the strike price you want to use and the date of expiration. It is suggested that to increase your profitability, and reduce the upfront costs, the strike price you must opt for must be closely related to the current trading price of the underlying asset.

Call Ratio Back Spread

You are required to purchase calls and the right calls to create a call ratio back spread. Since it is a ratio spread, the number of options you execute in each of these transactions will not be the same. As a rule of thumb, try to purchase two calls for every call you write. Always ensure that the total credit for the contracts you've written must be higher than the total debit for the contracts you have acquired.

Put Ratio Back Spread

You will earn a profit if the price of the underlying asset moves in either direction; however, your profitability increases if the price of the underlying asset's price goes down instead of going up. You are required to purchase puts and write puts simultaneously. As is obvious, both of these transactions will be based on the same underlying asset. The only difference is that instead of purchasing an equal number of puts, you will be purchasing to puts for every put you right. The puts you purchase must be at the money while the ones you write must be in the money. The expiry date, along with the underlying security, must be the same.

Short Calendar Call Spread

The strategy is best used when you are certain that there will be a significant price movement in the value of the underlying security. However, you are uncertain of the direction in which the security will swing. Instead of spending a lot of time trying to analyze the direction of the price change, you can use the strategy. The strategy is likely complicated, and beginners must not attempt it on the first try. There are two transactions you must make.

The first transaction is to purchase at the money calls, and the second transaction is to write at the money calls. Since it is a calendar spread, the expiry date is used for both these transactions must be different. The options you decide to purchase must be short-term with a relatively close expiry date while the options you write must be long term with a longer date of expiration.

Short Calendar Put Spread

Two transactions are required to execute this strategy- purchase at the money puts while writing at the money puts. The date of expiration for both these transactions will be different since it is a calendar spread. The price of the contracts that have a longer expiry date will be quite high as compared to the ones with a shorter expiration date. It is based on the basic idea that a substantial movement in the value of the underlying security will mean that the extrinsic value of both sets of options will end up being equal or close to being full. The initial credit you receive is because of the higher extrinsic value of the options written. So, if the extrinsic value becomes equal on both sites, then that credit that will be created is your profits.

CHAPTER 10:

Strangles and Straddles

O ptions allow you to create strategies that simply are not possible when investing in stocks. One strategy that we are going to discuss is earning a profit, no matter which way the stock moves. There are two ways that you can do this, they are known as strangles and straddles. This is a more complicated strategy than merely buying a long call option or a long put. But it's not that complicated; you just have to understand some basics on how to set them up to make a profit.

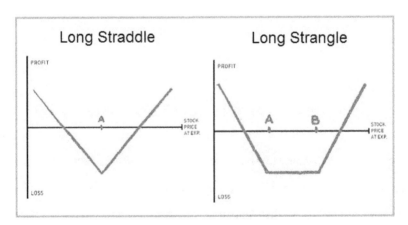

The strategy that is used in this case is dependent on a significant move by the stock. There are many situations where this might be appropriate. But mainly, this is something you will consider using when you are looking to profit from an earnings call.

Earning calls cause major price shifts in the big stocks. The price shift is mostly determined by what the analyst's "expectations" are for earnings, and so this is not always a rational process. If the company beats the analyst expectations when it comes to earnings per share, this creates a positive "surprise" that will usually send the stock soaring. The amount of "surprise" is given by the percentage difference between the actual value and the expected value. So, in this case, if you had bought a call option, you could make incredible levels of profit from the option by selling it in the next day or two, as long as the new higher price level is maintained.

But the problem is, you have no idea beforehand whether the earnings are going to exceed or fail to meet the analyst expectations. The silly thing about this (from a common-sense perspective) is that even if the company is profitable if they fail to meet analyst expectations, this results in massive disappointment. So, you might see share prices drop from a sell-off even if the company is profitable. This is "surprise" in a negative way.

The impact of failing to meet expectations can be magnified if the company also has some bad news to share. A recent example we mentioned was an earnings call from Netflix, where they revealed that over the past quarter, they had lost subscribers. This news hit Netflix stock hard, and it dropped by a walloping $42. If you had purchased a put option, that could have meant a $4000 profit.

The problem is that you don't know ahead of time which way the stock is going to go. It's one thing to look back and say well you could have had a put option and made $4k in a day, but often companies reveal information in earnings calls that have been under wraps. Nobody had any inkling that Netflix was going to be losing subscribers until the earnings call.

Second, analyst expectations are somewhat arbitrary. Defining success or failure in terms of them is pretty silly, but that is the way things work right now. But the point is it's impossible to know whether these unreasonable expectations are met before the earnings call. It's also impossible to gauge the level of reaction that is going to be seen from exceeding or failing to meet expectations.

Since we don't know which way the stock is going to move, it would seem that an excellent strategy to use is to buy a call and a put at the same time. That is precisely the idea behind a straddle and a strangle.

That way, you profit no matter what happens, as long as the price on the market changes somewhat sharply in one direction or another. When you set up a straddle or a strangle, there is a middle "red zone" that bounds the current share price over which you are going to lose money. But if the share price either goes above the boundaries of this zone or below it, you will make profits.

If the stock shoots upward, this means that the put option is going to drop massively in value. So, it's a write-off for you. But if the stock makes a strong move, as they often do after positive earnings calls, you stand to make enough profits from the call option that was a part of your trade to more than make up for the loss of the put. The potential upside gain is, in theory, unlimited. Of course, in practice, share prices don't rise without limit, but they might increase, $10, $20, or $40, and that could potentially earn profits of roughly $1,000-$4,000, more than covering any loss from the now worthless put option.

The opposite situation applies, as well. If the stock drops by a significant amount, you make profits. Profits to the downside are capped because a stock price cannot decline below zero. That said, if the stock drops by a significant amount, you can still make hundreds to thousands of dollars per contract virtually overnight.

Doing this requires some attention on your part. You are going to have to think ahead to implement this strategy and profit from it. Remember that you can use a straddle or strangle any time that you consider the stock is going to make a significant shift one way or the other. An example of a non-earning season situation, where this could be a useful strategy, would be a new product announcement. Think Apple. If Apple is having one of their big presentations, if the new phone that comes out disappoints the analysts, share prices are probably going to drop by a significant amount. On the other hand, if it ends up surprising viewers with a lot of new features that make it the must-have phone again, this will send Apple stock soaring.

The problem here is you don't know which way it's going to go. There are going to be leaks and rumors but basing your trading decisions on that is probably not the right approach, often, the rumors are wrong. A strangle or straddle kind allows you to avoid that kind of situation and make money either way.

Other situations that could make this useful are either changes in management or any political interaction. We mentioned the government recently made a privacy settlement with Facebook. If you knew when the agreement was going to occur but wasn't sure what it was going to be, using a strangle or straddle might be an excellent way to earn money from the significant price moves that were sure to follow.

The same events that might warrant buying a long call, such as a GDP number or jobs report, for options on index funds, are also appropriate for strangles and straddles.

CHAPTER 11:

Credit Spreads and Debit Spreads Explained

The use of spreads is another tactical approach to options trading. The spread is described as the acquisition and sale of two different options with the same associate asset attached.

Credit spreads describe the selling of a high-premium option at the same time acquiring a low-premium option in a similar class (calls or puts). This results in a credit to the investor's account. Both of these options have the same expiration date but different strike prices. The aim here is to make a profit when the spread between the two options becomes narrowed.

On the other hand, a debit spread is one where the trader buys a high-premium option and sells a low-premium option with the same associated asset attached to both options. Just like with a credit spread, both options have the same expiration date but different strike prices. The trader makes a profit when the spread between the two options widens. This results in a debit to the trader's account.

Credit Spreads

A credit spread is advantageous because the seller collects more in premium than what is paid out in the options. For example, if the trader sells an option for $1000 and buys another option at a lower strike price of $75 then they will have a net result of $25. We refer to this as a credit because they are collecting more than they are paying out.

There are several types of credit spreads, but we will focus on 2—the put credit spread and the call credit spread. The put credit spread has a bullish outlook and relies on time decay. The profit comes when the stock prices increase. Profit for 100 shares of stock is calculated with this formula:

- Credit Received x 100 = Profit

The loss for 100 shares of stock is calculated with this formula:

- (Width of the two Strike Prices - Credit Received) x 100 = Loss

Breakeven is calculated with this formula:

- Short Put Strike Price - Credit Received = Breakeven

The call credit spread is approached with a bearish outlook and it too relies on time decay. Profits are realized when stock prices decrease. Profit for 100 shares of stock is calculated with this formula:

- Credit Received x 100 = Profit

The loss for 100 shares of stock is calculated with this formula:

- (Width of the two Strike Prices - Credit Received) x 100 = Loss

Breakeven is calculated with this formula:

- Short Call Strike Price - Credit Received = Breakeven

Types of Credit Spreads

- Bull Put Spread: This is a great options strategy for beginners to implement. It is a bearish technique that relies on the price of the associated asset going down significantly enough but not by a huge jump. Two transactions are required with an upfront cost. The trader:
  - Buys 1 out of the money put
  - Sells 1 on the money put

They are implemented by buying a lower-premium out of the money put option while simultaneously selling one in the money put option that is of a higher premium.

Profit is achieved when the price of the associated asset is equal to the credit received from the options.

The formula for this is:

- Premium Received - Commissions Paid = Profit

Loss occurs when the stock prices go below the strike price on or before the expiration date. This is calculated with this formula:

- Strike Price of Short Put - Strike Price of Long Put Net Premium + Commissions Paid = Loss

Breakeven is calculated like this:

- Strike Price of Short Put - Net Premium Received = Breakeven

Bear Call Spread: This type of option works similarly to the one stated above, and profit is reliant on the prices of the associated asset falling moderately. The trader:

- Buys 1 out of the money call
- Sells 1 in the money call

Profit is calculated with this formula:

- Premium Received - Commissions Paid = Profit

Loss occurs when the stock prices go above the strike price on or before the expiration date. This is calculated with this formula:

- Strike Price of Long Call - Strike Price of Short Call-Net Premium Received + Commissions Paid = Loss

Breakeven is calculated like this:

- Strike Price of Short Call + Net Premium Received = Breakeven

This bearish strategy is slightly more complicated and is not typically recommended for novice options traders. Short Butterfly Spread: This is a volatility-based strategy that is typically practiced by medium to advanced options traders. This applies to both call and put options of this type. Three transactions are involved. They are:

- Buying 1 in the money call/put
- Selling 1 out of the money call/put
- Buying 1 as the money call/put

This is not an options trading strategy that a trader should jump into lightly. This requires careful thought and consideration. Thus, this is a strategy that is best employed by intermediate and advanced options traders. However, when done right, this strategy offers benefits like increased flexibility and the ability to profit no matter which direction the price of the asset goes. Both the profit and loss of this type of strategy are limited. This limitation is great for managing risks.

Iron Butterfly Spread: This is a neutral strategy that entails 4 transactions. The trader:

- Buys 1 out of the money call
- Sells 1 at the money call
- Buys 1 out of the money put
- Sells 1 at the money put

The two calls and puts of this options strategy are equal and the associated asset and expiration date of all of these components are the same. Due to the complexity of this strategy, it is not suitable for beginners. The higher commissions also make it less appealing to most traders. However, the benefits include a higher potential profit. This strategy is useful for making a huge payout. Thus, on such a sizable contract, the commission increase may be worth pursuing this strategy.

Pros and Cons of Credits Spreads

One of the biggest advantages of using credit spreads is that they drastically lower the risk to the trader if the stock price moves against the trader. Next, the seller receives cash upfront in the form of premium payment. Losses are limited because the trader stands to benefit no matter what direction the price of the associated asset moves.

The biggest disadvantage of this type of option strategy is that it requires a trader to use a margin account. This is not something a trader might necessarily want to do. Also, another disadvantage is even though the losses are limited so are the profits.

Debit Spreads

Unlike a credit spread where the seller receives cash into his or her account, debit spreads instead carry an upfront cost. The premium is paid from the investor's account when the position is opened, and this is referred to as a debit. This type of strategy is mostly used to offset the costs associated with having long option positions. This results because the premium received from long components is more than the premium received from short components. As a result of this, the net debt is the highest possible value for loss in this type of option strategy. Losses are thus limited.

Despite this upfront cost, debit spreads are generally considered safer to create and less complicated than credit spreads. Debit spreads are therefore more commonly used by beginners compared to credit spreads. Just like the credit spreads, there are at least two options involved in the transaction. The trader pays for a higher premium option while selling a lower-premium option. However, just like with credit spreads the number of transactions executed in this strategy can exceed 2.

Just like with credit spreads, there are call and put versions. The basic call version is set up like this — the investor:

- Buys 1 call
- Sells 1 call (this is the higher strike)

Profit is calculated with this formula:

- Width of the two Strike Prices – Premium – Commissions = Profit

Loss is calculated with this formula:

- Premium Paid + Commissions = Loss

With the put option, the set up looks like this:

- Sell 1 put
- Buy 1 put (this is the higher strike)

Profit is calculated with this formula:

- Width of the two Strike Prices – Premium – Commissions = Profit

Loss is calculated with this formula:

- Premium Paid + Commissions = Loss

All of these equations will be x100 to prepare a contract with 100 shares as the associated asset.

Types of Debit Spreads

Bull Call Spread: This is a relatively simple strategy to implement as it only requires 2 transactions. The trader:

- Buys 1 at the money call
- Sells 1 out of money call

This is a bullish strategy that is implemented when the trader believes that the price of the associated asset will rise moderately.

Profit is achieved when the price of the associated asset is equal to the strike prices of the short call. The formula for this is:

- Strike Price of Short Call - Strike Price of Long = Profit

Loss occurs when the stock price goes below the strike price on or before the expiration date. This is calculated with this formula:

- Net Premium Paid + Commissions Paid = Loss

Breakeven is calculated like this:

- Strike Price of Long Call + Net Premium Paid = Breakeven

Bear Put Spread: This is a bearish strategy that is used when a trader believes that the price of the associated asset will go down by a moderate amount.

It only requires 2 transactions and is, therefore, suitable for beginners. The trader:

- Buys 1 at the money put
- Sells 1 on the money put

This is a straightforward strategy that has limited losses and profits with comparatively low upfront costs.

Profit is achieved when the price of the associated asset is equal to the strike prices of the short call. The formula for this is:

- Width of the two Strike Prices - Net Premium Paid - Commissions Paid = Profit

Loss occurs when the stock price goes above the strike price on or before the expiration date. This is calculated with this formula:

- Net Premium Paid + Commissions Paid = Loss

Breakeven is calculated like this:

- Strike Price of Long Put + Net Premium Paid = Breakeven

Reverse Iron Butterfly:

This is a volatile strategy that is used when a trader believes that the price of the associated asset will move sharply at price but is not sure in which direction.

Thus, this strategy is created to gain a profit no matter the direction.

It requires 4 transactions and they are:

- Sell 1 out of money put
- Buy 1 at the money put
- Buy 1 at the money call
- Sell 1 out of money call

The profit gained in this type of strategy is limited and is achieved when the associated asset price drops below the strike price.

The formula for this is:

- Width of the two Strike Prices - Net Premium Paid - Commissions Paid = Profit

Loss occurs when the stock price is the same as the strike price on the expiration date. This is calculated with this formula:

- Net Premium Paid + Commissions Paid = Loss

The 2 breakeven points for this strategy are calculated like this:

- Strike Price of Long Call + Net Premium Paid = Breakeven
- Strike Price of Long Put + Net Premium Paid = Breakeven

Butterfly Spread: This is a neutral strategy that involves 3 transactions. The trader:

- Buys 1 in the money call
- Sells 2 at the money calls
- Buys 1 on the money call

The profit gained in this type of strategy is limited and is achieved when the associated asset price remains unchanged on the expiration date. The formula for this is:

- Width of the two Strike Prices - Net Premium Paid - Commissions Paid = Profit

Loss is also limited. It occurs when the stock price is the same as the strike price on the expiration date. This is calculated with this formula:

- Net Premium Paid + Commissions Paid = Loss

The 2 breakeven points for this strategy are calculated like this:

- Strike Price of Higher Strike Long Call - Net Premium Paid = Breakeven
- Strike Price of Lower Strike Long Call + zNet Premium Paid = Breakeven

This is not a strategy that is recommended for beginners, but it can indeed bring in a high return on investment. Unfortunately, because of the higher number of transactions, the commissions paid on this strategy can be high.

Pros and Cons of Debit Spreads

The benefits of debits spread include:

- They aid in trade planning because they help the trader determined potential maximum profits and losses in advance.
- Losses are limited due to how these types of strategies are implemented.
- Margin accounts are not required for this type of option strategy and can be used by traders who cannot use them.
- They offer greater profit margins.

There are also disadvantages to these types of options strategies. The biggest is that the profit margin is limited just as the losses are limited.

CHAPTER 12:

Iron Condor Explained and Examples

This options trading strategy is similar to the iron butterfly and has 4 transactions. The two strategies are mistaken for each other, but the iron condor allows for a great profit margin. This is a result of the iron butterfly spread requiring the associated asset to be the same price to take maximum profit while the iron condor allows for a range to reach the profit margin. The downside of this is that the maximum profit that can be earned is lowered. The particulars of the iron condor are:

- **Strategy type:** Neutral
- **Trader Level:** Advance
- **Spread type:** Credit

This options strategy requires 4 transactions. The trader has to:

- Sell 1 out of the money put
- Buy 1 out of the money put (has the lower strike)
- Sell 1 out of the money call
- Buy 1 out of the money call (has the higher strike)

All four options have the same expiration date.

The maximum profit available from this options strategy is equal to the net credit that is received upon entering the contract. Profit is earned when the associated asset prices at the expiration date fall between the call and put that are sold.

The formula to calculate this looks like this:

- Net Premium Received - Commissions Paid = Profit

The loss experienced with this strategy is limited and non-directional because this strategy is comparative to combining a bear call spread and a bull put spread. Loss is calculated with this formula:

- Width of the two Strike Prices - Net Premium Received + Commissions Paid = Loss

Unfortunately, the loss can be a lot higher than the profit with this strategy because it can occur either when the price of the associated asset falls at or below the lower strike of the put or if it rises above or is equal to the higher strike of the call.

There are 2 breakeven points. Breakeven is calculated with these formulas:

- Strike Price of Short Call + Net Premium Received = Breakeven
- Strike Price of Short Put - Net Premium Received = Breakeven

Benefits of the Iron Condor Spread

- The stock can go in any direction and the trader can still make a profit.
- This is a flexible strategy that allows for minimizing risk while still potentially earning the trader profits every month.
- Profit can be made with a broad range at the date of expiration.
- These are short-term contracts so profits can be realized in 3 months or less.
- The investor can make predeterminations of what the potential losses and profits can be before entering the contract.

Risks of the Iron Condor Spread

The biggest disadvantage of this strategy is its complexity. The 4 legs mean that this is a strategy that is best suited for advanced traders. This means that any trader who does not understand options on the level needed or understands the financial market stands to makes a loss if he or she implements this strategy incorrectly.

A great alternative to the iron butterfly spread, this options strategy is great if a trader is trying to gain a profit from having a neutral outlook. It has for legs, which look like this:

- Sell 1 out of the money put
- Buy 1 out of the money put (has the lower strike)
- Sell 1 out of the money call
- Buy 1 out of the money call (has the higher strike)

Maximum profit is achieved when the associated asset price at the expiration date falls between the call and put that is sold. This is a strategy best left to advanced options traders.

CHAPTER 13:

Common Mistakes Not to
Do in Options Trading

Mistakes happen in every field, sector, and industry. Some are always anticipated, while others happened unexpectedly. When it comes to stock trading, there are several mistakes that you can make. Understanding these mistakes can help you avoid them, thus ending up successful in your stock investments. Here are some of the common mistakes made by most investors, beginners, and professional traders alike:

Failure to Understand the Trade

It is always wrong to invest in a trade or business you know nothing about. It is a great mistake to engage in stock trading when you do not understand the business and financial models involved. You can avoid this mistake by taking the time to research the stock market and stock trading before investing your money. Know the different markets, the driving forces, as well as trading procedures.

Most investors tend to buy stocks from the latest companies and industries they know very little about. Although such companies may look promising, it is difficult to determine whether they will continue to exist. Understanding a specific company gives you a better hand over other investors. You will be able to make accurate predictions about the company or industry, which may bring you more profit. You will quickly tell when the business is booming, stagnating, or closing way before other investors get this information. Individuals who do not take time to study companies miss out on future trends of these companies. Failing to establish such trends leads to several missed opportunities. For instance, a person who invests in a company that is higher than his capital may quickly lose all his investment.

That is why it is always advisable that you invest in the industry you understand better. For instance, if you are a surgeon, you can invest in stocks that deal with medicine or related stocks. Lawyers can invest in companies that generate income through litigation, and so on.

Impatience

The stock market is for patient investors. It is a slow but steady form of investment. Although it bears various opportunities that can bring you money, you cannot make enough profit in one day. Most stock investors are always faced with the challenge of being patient. Some end up losing trade positions before they mature in the quest to make quick money. Exiting the market too early will always cost you some returns. As a new investor, you must never expect your investment portfolio to perform more than its capability, as this will always lead to a disaster. Remain realistic in terms of the time, duration, and resources needed to earn from the market.

Failure to Diversify

Another mistake that easily causes disaster is the failure to diversify. Professional investors do not have a problem with this since they can easily profit from a single type of stock. However, young investors must be able to diversify to secure their investment. Some of them do not stick to this principle.

Most of these lose a great fortune as soon as they get onto the stock market.

As you seek to invest, remember the rule of thumb governing stock diversity. This states that you should not invest more than 10% of your capital in one type of stock.

Getting Too Connected with a Certain Company

The essence of trading in stock is to make a profit. Sometimes, investors get too deep into a certain company that they forget that it is all about the shares and not the company itself. Being too attached to a company may cloud your judgment when it comes to stock trading since you may end up buying stocks from this company instead of getting the best deal on the market. As you learn more about companies, always remember that you are into the business to make money, besides creating relationships.

Investment Turnover

Investment turnover refers to the act of entering and exiting positions at will. This is one other mistake that destroys great investments. It is only beneficial to institutions that seek to benefit from low commission rates. Most stock trading positions charge transaction fees. The more frequently you buy and sell, the more you pay in terms of transaction fees. You, therefore, need to be careful when entering positions. Do not get in or exit too early. Have a rough idea of when you want to close positions so that you do not miss some of the long-term benefits of these positions.

Timing the Market

Market timing results in high investment turnover. It is not easy to successfully time the market. On average, only 94% of stock trading returns are acquired without the use of market timing. Most traders time the market as a way of attempting to recover their losses. They want to get even by making some profit to count a loss. This is always known as a cognitive error in behavioral finance. Trying to get even on the stock market will always result in double losses.

Trading with Emotions

Allowing your emotions to rule is one of the things that kill your stock investment returns. Most people get into the market for fear of losses or thirst to make returns too fast. As a young trader, you must ensure that greed and fear do not overwhelm your decision making. Stock prices may fluctuate a lot in the short-term; however, this may not be the case in the long term, especially for large-cap stocks. This means that you may get lower profits in the short-term, but these may increase in the long-term. Understanding this will help you avoid closing trades when it is not the right time yet.

Setting Unrealistic Expectations

This always occurs when dealing with small-cap stocks such as penny stocks. Most investors buy such stocks with the expectation that the prices will change drastically. Sometimes this works, but it is not a guarantee. To make great fortunes, people invest a lot of capital in these stocks, and then the prices do not change much. If these investors are not prepared for such an eventuality, they may feel frustrated and may quit the business completely. However, this is something that you must be able to manage if you want to grow your investment. Do not expect more than what a certain type of stock can deliver.

Using Borrowed Money

This is probably one of the greatest mistakes that investors make. Some investors get carried away with the returns they are making. As a way of getting more profits, they borrow money and use it to enter more stock positions. This is a very dangerous move and can result in a lot of stress. Stock trading is like gambling. You are not always sure how much you take home at the end of each trade. It is therefore not advisable for you to invest borrowed money in it.

As you try to avoid these mistakes, you must also avoid getting information from the wrong sources. Some traders have lost a fortune because they relied on the wrong sources for stock information. It is important to isolate a small number of people and places where you will seek guidance from. Do not be a person that follows the crowd. Take time before investing in new stock opportunities. Carry out proper due diligence, especially with small-cap stocks since these involve a lot of risks. Remember, you must trade carefully and implement expert advice if you want to succeed in stock trading.

Conclusion

Thank you for making it through to the end of the Options Trading Crash Course, let's hope it was informative and able to provide you with all of the tools you need to achieve your goals whatever they may be.

Options trading is a very exciting part of the stock market. With options trading, you can control large amounts of stock without actually owning it. This means that you can earn profits from movements in the stock price without risking huge amounts of capital. The return on investment on options is simply much better than the possible return on investment that you can earn trading options.

In this book, I have attempted to demystify options trading for you. We have explained what an option is, the difference between call and put options, and the strategies used by professional options traders when investing in options.

My hope is that rather than join the scare chorus that surrounds options from "financial advisors," I have shown you that options are actually a rational investment that can help you build your own successful trading business. Whether you engage in "speculation" or trading for investment income, options can help you read a six or even seven-figure income from your trading business, provided that you make careful trades and stick to the fundamental principles that are guaranteed to lead to success.

Your next steps are to actually get your feet wet with some trades. Start slowly, and spend some time trading small numbers of call and put options to build up some experience. Be sure to do both. Many novice traders are scared away from put options because they are not used to thinking in terms of earning money from declining stock prices. So, it's important to get over that and actually go through the experience of earning money while the company is having losses.

From there, you can start to employ options strategies after you've got a few months of experience making some trades. Before settling on a favorite, try the different strategies to see what you like best. Some people will end up focusing on only one trade. For example, many professional traders only trade iron condors, while others only sell put options. Others have a lot of variety and will engage in whatever trades suit them at the moment and what the market conditions are. This is a matter of personal taste, so you will have to figure out what works best for you.

I want to wish my readers good luck in the trading business!

CPSIA information can be obtained
at www.ICGtesting.com
Printed in the USA
BVHW090823070521
606415BV00005BA/1524